51305583 2

MONSTER MATHS

SHAPES

WRITTEN BY

MADELINE TYLER

ILLUSTRATED BY

AMY LI

BookLife
PUBLISHING

©2019
BookLife Publishing Ltd.
King's Lynn
Norfolk PE30 4LS

ISBN: 978-1-78637-580-3

Written by:
Madeline Tyler

Edited by:
John Wood

Designed/Illustrated by:
Amy Li

PHOTO CREDITS

All images courtesy of Shutterstock. With thanks to Getty Images, Thinkstock Photo and iStockphoto.

Cover, Page 1 & Page 2 – memphisslim, jojje, Dmitrijj Skorobogatov, Abscent. Master Images – jojje (grid), Dmitrijj Skorobogatov (illustration texture), Abscent (pattern), ag1100 (paper), Corey Frey (Dot texture), Amy Li (all illustrations). Dot's room – arigato, ag1100, cluckva, NataliaStr, Svjatoslav Andreichyn, wk1003mike. 4-5 – GraphiTect, fluke samed, Alexander Mazurkevich, Kriengsuk Prasroetsung, Draw05, happystock, Ratchat, wk1003mike, Forkagraphy. 8-9 – fluke samed, GalapagosPhoto, Gita Kulinitch Studio, iliveinoctober, 12-13 – sripfoto, Sofia Iartseva, Abstractor, Alexander Mazurkevich, Draw05, happystock, 16-17 – Forkagraphy, 20-21 – wk1003mike, Podsolnukh, Ratchat, Kriengsuk Prasroetsung, 24 – wk1003mike, ag1100.

Shapes are
all around us!

4

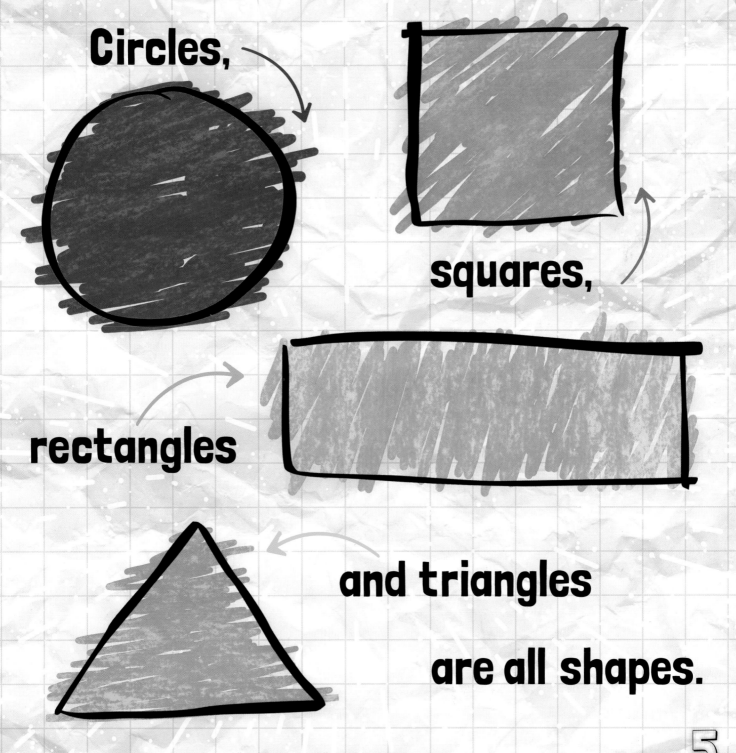

Circles,

squares,

rectangles

and triangles

are all shapes.

5

This is
a CIRCLE.

Circles have one SIDE

and no CORNERS.

The SUN is a circle.

BALLOONS can

be circles, too.

9

This is a TRIANGLE.

Triangles have three SIDES and three CORNERS.

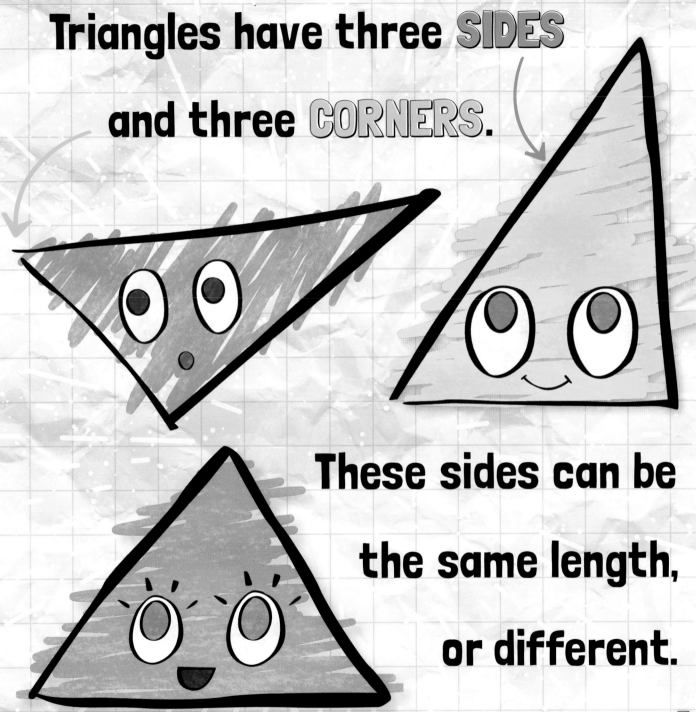

These sides can be the same length, or different.

11

SANDWICHES can be triangles.

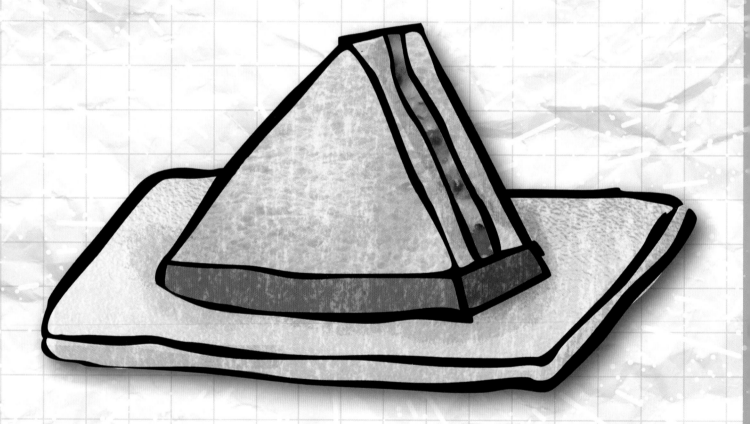

Some TREES look like triangles.

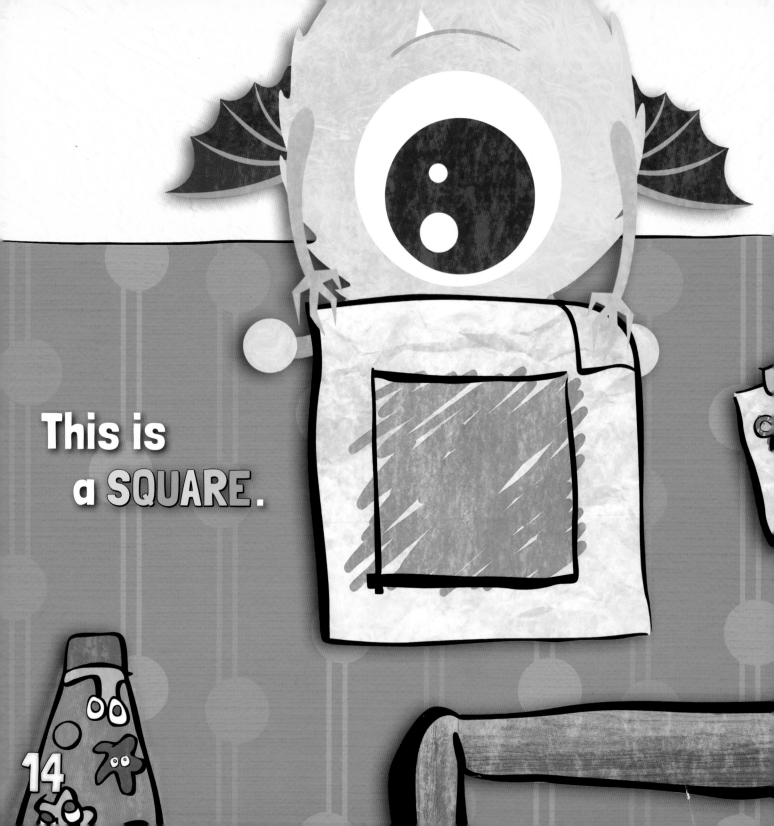

This is
a SQUARE.

14

Squares have four SIDES and four CORNERS.

All the sides are the same length.

Your WINDOWS might be square.

This BOOK is square.

MONSTER MATHS

SHAPES

This is
a RECTANGLE.

18

Rectangles have four SIDES and four CORNERS.

Two of the sides are longer,

and two of the sides are shorter.

Are the **DOORS** in your house rectangles?

20

RULERS are

very long rectangles.

Dot has drawn
lots of shapes!

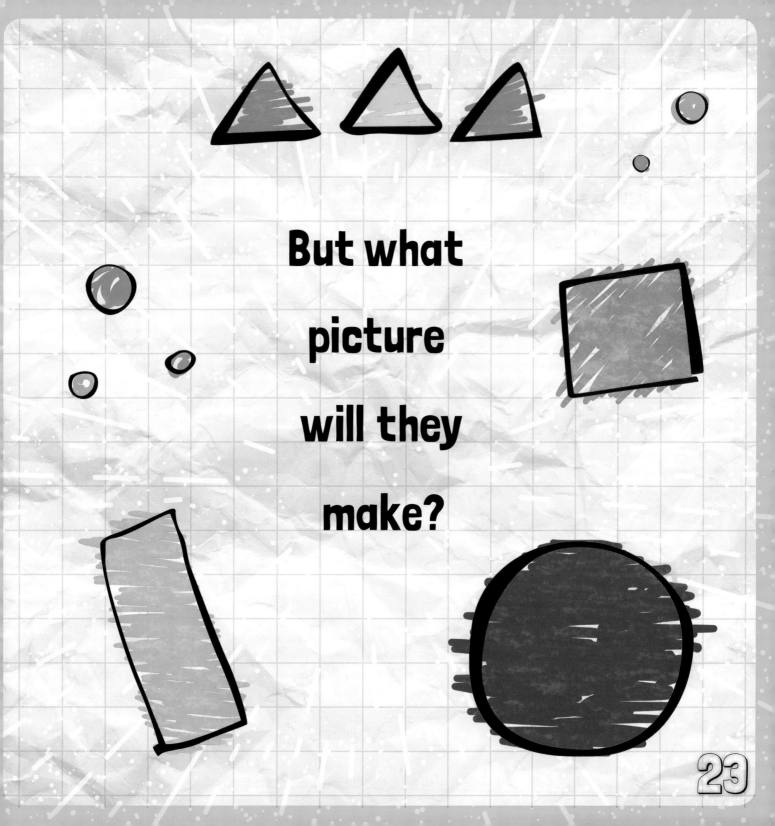

But what
picture
will they
make?

23